100 First Words
for Toddlers
幼児の初めての言葉100

English – Japanese Bilingual

英語/日本語バイリンガル

JAYME YANNUZZI

Translated by **Anna Sato**

Illustrations by **Sarah Rebar**

ROCKRIDGE
PRESS

Series Designer: Amanda Kirk
Interior and Cover Designer: Jami Spittler
Art Producer: Tom Hood
Editor: Laura Bryn Sisson
Production Editor: Andrew Yackira
Production Manager: Martin Worthington

Illustrations © Sarah Rebar

Paperback ISBN: 978-1-63807-029-0
    eBook ISBN: 978-1-63807-578-3
R0

To my daughter, whose first word, "Mama," was a memory I will never forget, even if it quickly turned to "duck." I love you. —J. Y.

わたしのむすめへ。あなたのはじめてのことばが『ママ』だったことはずっとわすれないわよ。すぐに『duck (ダック)』になっちゃったけどね。アイ・ラブ・ユー！ —J. Y.

To my mother, who lovingly taught me many Japanese words when I was young. Thank you! —A. S.

ちいさいときに にほんのことばをたくさんおしえてくれた やさしいおかあさんへ。ありがとう。 —A. S.

Dear Reader,

When you hear your toddler learn their first words, those are some of the most special memories you can make together! The best way for your child to learn is by interacting with you, so here are a few tips for how to use this book:

- Point to a picture on the page, say the word, and use it in a sentence.

- Ask questions about what your child notices on each page. You can say, "What are you pointing to? What do you see?"

- Play a game of *I Spy*. "I spy with my little eye . . . something yellow. Yes, a duck!"

- Have your toddler collect items around the house to match to the pictures in the book.

Use this book to read, talk, and play with your toddler over and over again.

Note: Children typically learn the hiragana character style first. However, in Japanese, loanwords from foreign languages are written in katakana. You will find both character styles in this book, depending on the word. In addition, each word is accompanied by rōmaji (romanization), which is commonly used in Japan to assist foreign travelers, as well as a syllable-by-syllable pronunciation aid in parentheses.

読者の皆様へ

子供のはじめての言葉を耳にした瞬間は誰にとっても忘れられない大切な親子の想い出となります。お子さんが最も効果的に言葉を学ぶには触れ合いが何よりも必要です。この本を使ってお子さんと次のように触れ合ってみてください。

- ページ内のイラストを指でさし、その言葉を単独で言ってあげたり、いろいろな文中でその言葉を使って言ってあげたりする。

- 各ページでお子さんが何に気づいたか聞いてあげる。例えば、「〇〇ちゃんが指でさしているのは何?」とか、「このページでは何が見えますか?」など。

- アイ・スパイのようなゲームをしてあげる。例えば、「何か黄色いものが見えますよ。何でしょうか。そう、そう!あひるさんです!」など。

- お子さんに本の中のイラストで示されている物を家の中で探して集めてもらう。

この本を使ってお子さんと『読む』、『話す』、『遊ぶ』を何度も繰り返してみてください。

注: 子供はたいてい片仮名の前に平仮名を学びます。しかし、外来語は片仮名で表記されます。ですから、本書では言葉によって平仮名か片仮名で表記しました。また、日本で外国人のために使用されているローマ字表記を加えましたが、括弧内に音節ごとに記した発音ガイドも添えました。

airplane
ひこうき
hikōki (hee-kohh-kee)

apple
りんご
ringo (reen-goh)

baby
あかちゃん
akachan (ah-kah-chahn)

ball
ボール
bōru (bohh-roo)

balloon

ふうせん

fūsen (fooo-sehn)

banana

バナナ

banana (bah-nah-nah)

bath
おふろ
ofuro (oh-foo-roh)

bed
ベッド
beddo (behd-doh)

belly
おなか
onaka (oh-nah-kah)

bib
よだれかけ
yodarekake (yoh-dah-reh-kah-keh)

bird
とり
tori (toh-ree)

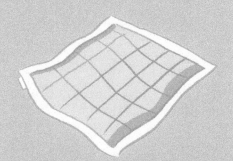

blanket
ブランケット
buranketto (boo-rahn-keht-toh)

blocks
つみき
tsumiki (tsoo-mee-kee)

boat
ふね
fune (foo-neh)

book
ほん
hon (hohn)

bookshelf
ほんだな
hondana (hohn-dah-nah)

bottle
ほにゅうびん
honyūbin (hoh-nyooo-been)

bowl
おちゃわん
ochawan (oh-chah-wahn)

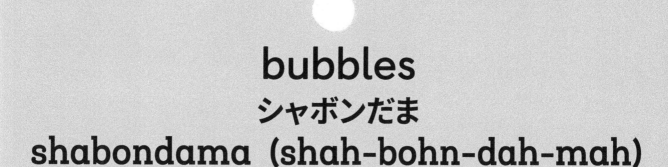

bubbles
シャボンだま
shabondama (shah-bohn-dah-mah)

bug
むし
mushi (moo-shee)

bunny
うさぎ
usagi (oo-sah-gee)

car
くるま
kuruma (koo-roo-mah)

carrot
にんじん
ninjin (neen-jeen)

cat
ねこ
neko (neh-koh)

cereal
シリアル
shiriaru (shee-ree-ah-roo)

chair
いす
isu (ee-soo)

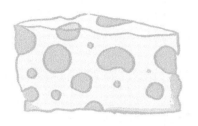

cheese
チーズ
chīzu (cheee-zoo)

chicken
にわとり
niwatori (nee-wah-toh-ree)

circle
まる
maru (mah-roo)

closet
クローゼット
kurōzetto (koo-rohh-zeht-toh)

coat
ジャンパー
jampā (jahm-pahh)

cookie
クッキー
kukkī (kook-keee)

couch
ソファー
sofā (soh-fahh)

cow
うし
ushi (oo-shee)

crayon
クレヨン
kureyon (koo-reh-yohn)

cup
コップ
koppu (kohp-poo)

diaper
おむつ
omutsu (oh-moo-tsoo)

dog
いぬ
inu (ee-noo)

doll
にんぎょう
ningyō (neen-gyohh)

door
ドア
doa (doh-ah)

drawer
ひきだし
hikidashi (hee-kee-dah-shee)

drink
のむ
nomu (noh-moo)

duck
あひる
ahiru (ah-hee-roo)

ears
みみ
mimi (mee-mee)

eat
たべる
taberu (tah-beh-roo)

eyes
め
me (meh)

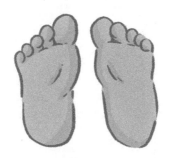

feet
あし
ashi (ah-shee)

flower
はな
hana (hah-nah)

fork
フォーク
fōku (fohh-koo)

grass
くさ
kusa (koo-sah)

happy
うれしい
ureshii (oo-reh-shee-ee)

hat
ぼうし
bōshi (bohh-shee)

head
あたま
atama (ah-tah-mah)

heart
ハート
hāto (hahh-toh)

house
いえ
ie (ee-eh)

juice
ジュース
jūsu (jooo-soo)

keys
かぎ
kagi (kah-gee)

lamp
でんき
denki (dehn-kee)

lion
ライオン
raion (rah-ee-ohn)

milk
ぎゅうにゅう
gyūnyū (gyooo-nyooo)

monkey
さる
saru (sah-roo)

mouth
くち
kuchi (koo-chee)

neck
くび
kubi (koo-bee)

noodles
めん
men (mehn)

nose
はな
hana (hah-nah)

pants
ズボン
zubon (zoo-bohn)

paper
かみ
kami (kah-mee)

park
こうえん
kōen (kohh-ehn)

peas
グリンピース
gurinpīsu (goo-reen-peee-soo)

pig
ぶた
buta (boo-tah)

pillow
まくら
makura (mah-koo-rah)

plate
おさら
osara (oh-sah-rah)

play
あそぶ
asobu (ah-soh-boo)

potty
おまる
omaru (oh-mah-roo)

sad
かなしい
kanashii (kah-nah-shee-ee)

shirt
シャツ
shatsu (shah-tsoo)

shoe

くつ

kutsu (koo-tsoo)

shorts

ショートパンツ

shōtopantsu (shohh-toh-pahn-tsoo)

sleep
ねる
neru (neh-roo)

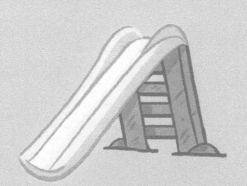

slide
すべりだい
suberidai (soo-beh-ree-dah-ee)

socks
くつした
kutsushita (koo-tsoo-shee-tah)

spoon
スプーン
supūn (soo-pooon)

square
しかく
shikaku (shee-kah-koo)

stairs
かいだん
kaidan (kah-ee-dahn)

star
ほし
hoshi (hoh-shee)

strawberry
いちご
ichigo (ee-chee-goh)

stroller
ベビーカー
bebīkā (beh-beee-kahh)

swing
ブランコ
buranko (boo-rahn-koh)

switch
スイッチ
suitchi (soo-eet-chee)

table
テーブル
tēburu (tehh-boo-roo)

teddy bear
テディーベア
tedībea (teh-deee-beh-ah)

towel
タオル
taoru (tah-oh-roo)

train
トレイン
torein (toh-reh-een)

tree
き
ki (kee)

triangle
さんかく
sankaku (sahn-kah-koo)

truck
トラック
torakku (toh-rahk-koo)

umbrella
かさ
kasa (kah-sah)

wagon
カート
kāto (kahh-toh)

walk
あるく
aruku (ah-roo-koo)

window
まど
mado (mah-doh)

About the Author

Jayme Yannuzzi, M. Elementary Ed., is a former first-grade teacher and the creator of the blog *Teach Talk Inspire*, where she shares resources to entertain and educate kids at home.

About the Illustrator

Sarah Rebar is an illustrator based in Los Angeles, with a BFA in Illustration and Design from Syracuse University. She loves to draw stories and fun illustrations for kids.

About the Translator

Anna Sato is a coauthor of *My First Japanese Kanji Book* (Tuttle, 2009) and *Japanese Folktales for Language Learners* (Tuttle, forth-coming). She grew up bilingual and was co-president of the Japan Society at Harvard University.

CPSIA information can be obtained
at www.ICGtesting.com
Printed in the USA
JSHW050811200921
18778JS00001BA/1